The
WIREWORKER'S
•COMPANION•

Denise Peck & Jane Dickerson

W9-ATF-689

INTERWEAVE.
interweave.com

WITHDRAWN

Editor
Erica Smith

Associate Art Director
Julia Boyles

Cover + Interior Designer
Adrian Newman

Photographer
Jim Lawson, except where noted

Production Designer
Katherine Jackson

Library of Congress Cataloging-in-Publication Data not available at time of printing.

ISBN 978-1-59668-719-6 (spiral bound)

ISBN 978-1-59668-891-9 (PDF)

10 9 8 7 6 5 4 3 2 1

Interweave Press LLC
A division of F+W Media, Inc.
201 East Fourth Street
Loveland, CO 80537
interweave.com

Manufactured in China by RR Donnelley Shenzhen.

CONTENTS

INTRODUCTION

Welcome to *The Wireworker's Companion*. Inside you'll find everything you need to get started and grow your skills in wireworking: from the most basic tools and materials to fascinating advanced techniques, including examples of chain maille and weaving. Whether you are just starting out or wire is already your favorite medium, this book can be an invaluable resource. As our passion grew for wireworking, we felt the need for a reference guide, and we hope you'll find this a handy tool.

The versatility of wire makes it an ideal medium to work with in jewelry. Wireworking offers an abundance of beautiful materials you can work with in a wide range of textures, thicknesses, and hues. Very fine wire can produce delicate, elegant designs, and its soft malleability makes it very easy to work with. Heavier gauge wire can be hammered and textured and can result in dramatic, funky, chunky statement pieces. The beauty of working with wire is that you can make everything from a fine delicate finding to a bold, dramatic focal point. Add to that the unique qualities of different metals, including their responses to being oxidized and colorized, and the possibilities are truly endless.

It's easy to fall in love with wireworking, and we hope that as you build your skills and refine your techniques, this will be a book you will turn to again and again.

Denise Peck
Jane Dickerson

WIRE 101

In this chapter you will become more familiar with the basics of wire: What metal(s) it can be made of, the contrasting properties of each, and the many forms that wire can take.

METAL TYPES

Wire comes in a multitude of materials, giving you the flexibility of working within your price range. Base metals are inexpensive and readily available. Precious metals, such as silver and gold, are more expensive and can be found at jewelry suppliers. A great way to conserve on precious metals is to use them as accents with other less expensive metals, such as combining some sterling with copper.

BASE METAL refers to common and inexpensive metals such as iron, nickel, and copper. Base metals can also be alloys, or mixtures of these metals. And they all corrode and tarnish easily when exposed to air or moisture.

FERROUS METALS contain iron and therefore are magnetic. They corrode quite easily. Ferrous metals include steel and stainless steel.

NONFERROUS METALS, such as aluminum, copper, and tin, do not contain iron and are not magnetic. They resist corrosion more than ferrous metals.

PRECIOUS METALS are by definition relatively scarce and therefore expensive. In jewelry making, precious metals usually refer to gold, silver, and platinum. They're quite corrosion-resistant. And because they're a traded commodity, prices fluctuate constantly.

REACTIVE METALS, such as titanium and niobium, undergo a chemical reaction when combined with other elements. Niobium is a favorite for jewelry making. Originally silver/white, it turns beautiful rainbow colors in an anodizing process. It's a strong and nonallergenic metal.

WIRE TYPES

Each wire type has specific properties; some are soft and malleable and others are harder to manipulate. Knowing the properties of your wire is important before you begin working on a piece. Later in the book you will learn how to soften and harden your wire to suit your design.

> **TIP:** The purer the metal, the less it tarnishes. That's what gives fine silver and Argentium their antitarnish properties. Metal alloys, especially those that contain copper, are prone to tarnishing.

ALUMINUM wire is tarnish-resistant, lightweight, and very easy to manipulate. It comes in a variety of colors and gauges. Although the color is applied multiple times during the manufacturing process, it can scratch, and caution is needed when manipulating the wire with tools. Use Tool Magic rubber coating on your tools to prevent scratching or marring the finish of the aluminum.

ARGENTIUM wire is at least 93.5% silver and tarnish-resistant. It solders and fuses without oxidizing and yields a very high polish.

BRASS wire is a stiffer, harder metal, making it a bit more difficult to work with. It comes in two colors, yellow and red. Yellow brass wire is 60–70% copper and 30–40% zinc. Red brass wire has a warmer hue and is 85% copper and 15% zinc. Use patina to color brass instead of liver of sulfur, which only slightly dulls the color.

COPPER wire is inexpensive and great to use as practice wire. It is soft and malleable and comes in a variety of gauges. Sometimes the color can vary from spool to spool, so take note of that. Copper responds well to patina.

BRONZE wire is a copper alloy. It is stronger than copper and harder to work with. It is a warm golden color and can be darkened with liver of sulfur.

CRAFT wire is usually a copper core covered with a coating of color. It is soft and malleable and comes in a variety of colors and gauges. There are several brands of craft wire on the market. To avoid nicking the color coating when manipulating the wire, first cover your pliers' jaws in masking tape or Tool Magic.

FINE SILVER wire is 99.9% pure silver. It is soft and malleable, and it can be fused easily with a hand torch. It does not tarnish as quickly as sterling silver and does not oxidize in a flame. It can be oxidized in liver of sulfur or another blackening agent.

GERMAN-STYLE wire is nickel-free silver-plated copper wire with an antitarnish coating; it is also available in brass. It comes in a variety of gauges and shapes and has a medium temper, which is harder than craft wire and softer than half-hard sterling silver.

> **TIP:** If you don't know whether your wire is sterling or fine silver, hold a piece of the wire in a flame; if it turns black, it's sterling. If it doesn't turn black, it is fine silver.

GOLD wire is an alloy that does not tarnish. It is very expensive, and the amount of gold is measured in karats—the higher the number, the greater the percentage of gold.

GOLD-FILLED wire is made from layers of 12k or 14k gold that are bonded by heat and pressure to a brass base. It comes in a variety of gauges and hardnesses. Gold-filled is superior to gold-plated and will not chip or flake when manipulated. It looks like gold without the cost.

NICKEL SILVER wire is 18% nickel, 65% copper, and 17% zinc. It is sometimes referred to as German silver; however, it doesn't actually contain any silver. It is soft and malleable and comes in a variety of gauges. When polished, it has a silver-like appearance.

GOLD-PLATED AND SILVER-PLATED wire is copper wire plated with a thin coating of fine silver or gold. Often, plated wire has a baked-on clear coating to prevent tarnishing. It comes in a variety of gauges, shapes, and even colors. Plated wire is much more fragile than filled wire and, if uncoated, will scratch and flake.

NIOBIUM wire is hypoallergenic, strong, and corrosion-resistant. It is a very soft metal, so it is tempered to half-hard for jewelry making. It's naturally a silver color but is often anodized (coated with a protective film) to make it into a broad range of beautiful colors.

SILVER-FILLED wire has an outer layer of sterling silver surrounding a copper-alloy core. When cut, the end looks uniform, with no copper core showing. It has an antitarnish coating but does patina. It is available in a variety of gauges and hardnesses.

STAINLESS STEEL MEMORY wire is very hard and permanently coiled to "remember" its shape. It comes in stainless or carbon steel and is sold in different thicknesses and shapes. Never use fine- jewelry-making tools with memory wire because you can ruin them. Use a special memory-wire cutting tool.

STEEL wire is very inexpensive and can be found in hardware stores. It is a stiff metal requiring stronger tools and a special heavy-duty cutter. You can damage your fine-jewelry-making tools, so take care to use appropriate ones. Look for annealed steel wire, which is easier to work with. Steel wire rusts, so you need to coat the finished pieces with a wax or varnish.

STERLING SILVER wire is 92.5% silver and 7.5% copper and comes in a variety of gauges, shapes (round, half-round, square, twisted), and hardnesses. The copper in the wire oxidizes, and therefore the sterling wire will tarnish. Sterling responds well to patina.

TIP: *Keep your scraps of fine silver and sterling silver separate and sell them back to a jewelry supplier that offers this service such as Rio Grande (see Resources, page 109).*

WIRE SHAPES

ROUND wire is the easiest to obtain and most versatile. Its appearance is not affected by minor twisting. It can be intentionally twisted only by twisting two or more strands together.

HALF-ROUND wire is flat on one side and domed on the other. It is commonly used for ring shanks and also to lash together (flat-side down) a stack of wires.

SQUARE wire has a distinct appearance in jewelry because of its flat sides. Pieces laid side by side create an appearance of sheet metal. It can be twisted as a single strand (see Twisting Wire, page 57).

TRIANGULAR wire has three equal, flat sides. You can use it the same way you use half-round. It can also be twisted as a single strand.

RECTANGULAR wire is the easiest wire to use in making ring shanks or bracelets. It can also be used as stamping blanks.

Wire-shape chart

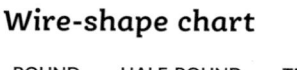

ROUND	HALF-ROUND	TRIANGLE	SQUARE

PATTERNED wire comes in a variety of prefabricated designs that can be oxidized to enhance the patterns. They are used to create rings, bracelets, dangles, and more.

TWISTED-PATTERNED wire looks like two wires twisted together but is in fact an imprinted patterned wire.

BEAD wire is another decorative wire and comes in full-bead (fully round) and half-bead (flat on one side).

TEMPER/HARDNESS

Temper defines the hardness of wire and is dead-soft, half-hard, or full-hard (or hard). You can change the temper of the wire by annealing (heating) it to soften the wire or hammering or tumbling it to stiffen (work-harden) it. (See Work-Hardening & Annealing on page 16.)

> **TIP:** *If you don't know what temper your wire is, give it a slight bend. If it doesn't spring back at all, it's dead-soft. If it springs back and retains its shape, it's half-hard (or hard, if you keep that in your stash).*

DEAD-SOFT is the easiest wire to work with but will not hold its shape. If you are weaving, coiling, or spiraling, you should work with dead-soft wire because it's much easier on the hands.

HALF-HARD has some spring-back to it and will hold its shape. If you're making ear wires or not planning on working the wire too much, start with half-hard or hard wire, which is already stiffer than dead-soft.

HARD OR FULL-HARD is the most difficult to manipulate and holds its shape. It's best for making bangles, chokers, cuffs, and any design where stiffness is an advantage.

WORK-HARDENING
& ANNEALING

WORK-HARDENING occurs when the wire is repeatedly bent or manipulated, causing it to become hard or stiff. Overworking a piece can cause the wire to become so brittle it breaks. Be mindful how much you are working the wire to avoid breakage. Work-hardening can also be a desirable effect when a soft piece of wire needs to be made stiffer to hold its shape. There are many ways to work-harden wire: straightening the wire with nylon-jaw pliers, gently hammering it with a ball-peen hammer and steel bench block, cleaning and straightening the wire with a polishing cloth, tumbling it in a rotary tumbler with steel shot, and bending and manipulating the wire.

ANNEALING is the process of heating wire or metal with a flame to a temperature at which it becomes soft and malleable. This can become necessary as you are working, for the metal work-hardens (grows stiffer and more resistant) the more it is manipulated.

Annealing usually occurs when the metal first glows red in the flame. At this point, immediately remove the flame and quench in a bowl of cool water. For more on annealing, see page 84.

GAUGE/SIZE

The size or diameter of the wire is known as the gauge. In the United States, the standard is Brown & Sharpe (B & S), also known as American Wire Gauge (AWG). The diameter of wire in inches or millimeters is translated into a numeral from 0 to 34; the higher the number, the thinner the wire.

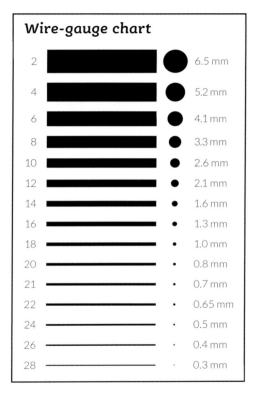

Wire-gauge chart

Gauge	Diameter
2	6.5 mm
4	5.2 mm
6	4.1 mm
8	3.3 mm
10	2.6 mm
12	2.1 mm
14	1.6 mm
16	1.3 mm
18	1.0 mm
20	0.8 mm
21	0.7 mm
22	0.65 mm
24	0.5 mm
26	0.4 mm
28	0.3 mm

TOOL TALK

Having the right tools for the task is essential in wireworking. In order not to damage your pliers or cutters, always make sure that you are not exceeding the manufacturer's guidelines for the gauge and material you are using. All these tools come in a wide range of price points, and more expensive does not necessarily mean better. Sometimes a hardware variety does the trick. The most important thing to remember is to choose tools that are comfortable for you and don't fatigue your hands.

MEASURING TOOLS

CALIPERS: Used to measure inner and outer diameters, calipers come in manual slide, digital, and dial varieties for reading measurements.

RULERS: Jewelry makers often use metric measurements. Your rulers should have both standard and metric measurements. Use straight rulers and tape measures to mark measurements in your work. To convert inches to millimeters, multiply by 25.4.

For example: 2" × 25.4 = 50.8 mm. To convert millimeters to inches, multiply by 0.03937.

For example: 25 mm × 0.03937 = 0.984".

WIRE GAUGE: The size or diameter of the wire is known as the gauge, but it also refers to the tool used to measure wire. Known as the Brown & Sharpe (B & S) wire gauge, this tool looks a bit like a flat, round gear. It measures the diameter of your wire and is an essential tool for wire jewelry making. A pocket gauge, which is smaller and has a slightly different shape, can be handy.

CUTTERS & SAWS

END CUTTERS: End cutters have blades perpendicular to the handles, providing more cutting leverage. These cutters require a little more pressure to cut and leave a slightly more noticeable burr on the end of the wire.

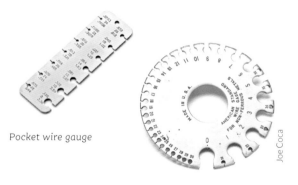

Pocket wire gauge

Standard wire gauge

Joe Coca

FLUSH CUTTERS/DIAGONAL CUTTERS/SIDE CUTTERS:
Flush cutters, diagonal cutters, and side cutters are all names for cutters that cut on their side. Flush cutters imply a smoother cut, leaving less of a burr on the end. They have pointed angled jaws that allow very close cuts in tight places. One side of the jaws is almost flat, the other is concave. Always hold the flat side of the cutters against your work and the concave side against the waste. The flat side creates a nice flush end on your work. Flush cutters are sold with a maximum gauge-cutting capacity; be sure to use cutters that can accommodate the wire you're using.

HEAVY-DUTY CUTTERS: Heavy-duty cutters are necessary when cutting heavy-gauge wire. Most heavy-duty cutters will cut to 12- or 11-gauge. Handles are usually ergonomic to prevent pain and injury when cutting such heavy wire. Never cut wire that is heavier than is recommended for the cutters.

ULTRAFLUSH CUTTERS: The unique ultraflush cutters leave a flat surface on cut ends, which virtually eliminates the "pinch" left by most cutters. This is valuable when you need an ultraclean cut, for example when you want a smooth join for jump rings. It has a more limited cutting range of gauges and greater possibility for edge damage due to misuse.

SAWS & BLADES: A jeweler's saw is a U-shaped handheld saw frame with clamps on either end. It is made to hold special serrated blades in an assortment of sizes. The frame is adjustable in length and depth to accommodate different sizes of working materials.

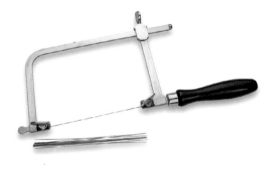

PLIERS

BAIL-FORMING PLIERS: Bail-forming pliers have long untapered jaws that enable you to make consistent loops. Each jaw is of a slightly different diameter, so one set of pliers enables you to make two sizes of loops.

BENT-NOSE PLIERS: Also called bent chain-nose pliers, these are similar to chain-nose pliers (see page 23) but have a bend at the tip that allows access to tight places for tasks such as tightening coils and tucking in ends. Two pairs used together are also helpful for opening and closing jump rings.

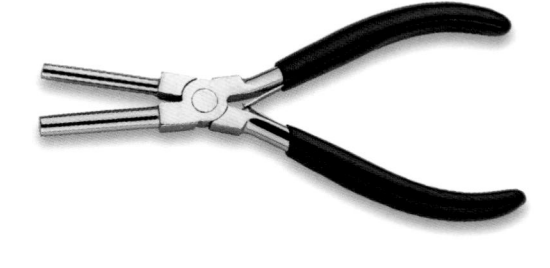

CHAIN-NOSE PLIERS: The workhorse of wire tools, chain-nose pliers are like needle-nose pliers (see page 25) but without teeth that can mar your wire. They are used for grasping wire, opening and closing jump rings, and making sharp angled bends. Because you may need to manipulate wire using both hands, it's a good idea to have at least two pairs in your workshop.

COIL-CUTTING PLIERS: This specialty tool was created to hold a coil of wire while you're sawing the coils into jump rings. You gently pinch the coil vertically between the jaws, and the slit down the side allows the insertion of the blade down the side of the coil.

FLAT-NOSE PLIERS: Flat-nose pliers have broad flat jaws and are good for making sharp bends in wire, grasping spirals, and holding components.

JUMP RING–CLOSING PLIERS: These bent-nose pliers have a small round channel in the jaws made for accessing tight spots and gripping and gently closing jump rings.

NEEDLE-NOSE PLIERS: Needle-nose pliers is the generic name for long-nose pliers with teeth, such as you'd find in your kitchen hardware drawer. Pliers with teeth should never be used when making jewelry, as the teeth will leave marks in the metal. They can be used as gripping pliers but not a forming or shaping tool, and only when that piece of the wire will be discarded.

NYLON-JAW PLIERS/WIRE-STRAIGHTENING PLIERS: The jaws of these pliers are made of hard nylon. Pulling wire through the clamped jaws will straighten any bends or kinks. They can also be used to hold, bend, or shape wire without marring the metal. Keep in mind that every time you pull wire through straightening pliers, you're work-hardening it more, making it more brittle and harder to manipulate.

NYLON-JAW FORMING PLIERS: This particular pair has one flat jaw and one conical jaw used to grip and form wire without marring it.

PARALLEL PLIERS: Parallel pliers are large, strong pliers that have jaws that remain parallel no matter how hard you manipulate them. They grip more tightly, and hold more securely, than other jeweler's pliers. They are perfect for holding wire securely when twisting.

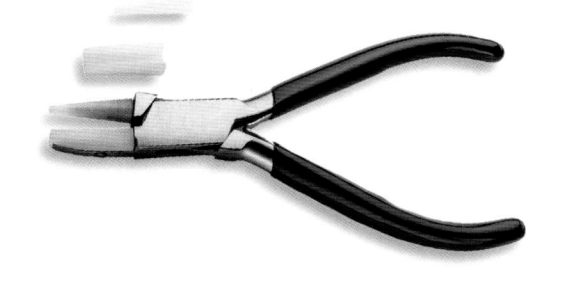

ROSARY PLIERS: These specialty pliers are made to form repetitive links on rosary chain. They are short-nosed, round-nose pliers with a built-in wire cutter.

ROUND-NOSE PLIERS: Another wireworker's necessity, round-nose pliers have pointed, graduated round jaws. They are used for making jump rings, simple loops, and curved bends in wire. They are also available in short and long nose. The longer the jaws of your pliers, the less force you can exert at the tip. Shorter jaws offer more strength at their tips, but less of a reach. Long jaws give you a long reach, but less leverage at the tips. You can ruin long-jawed pliers trying to bend heavy-gauge wire.

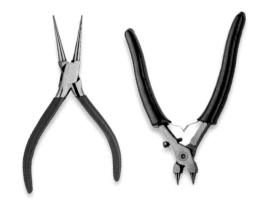

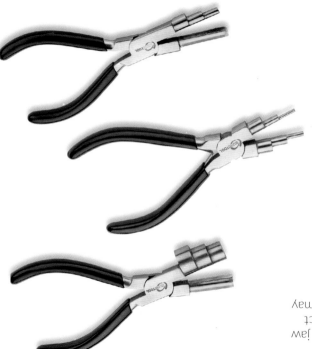

STEPPED FORMING PLIERS: Stepped forming pliers come in different sizes and shapes. They can have one flat jaw or one concave jaw and one of various-sized round barrels. They're perfect for wrapping loops of a consistent size. They may also be called wrap-and-tap pliers.

MANDRELS & WIRE-SHAPING TOOLS

MANDRELS: A mandrel is a spindle, rod, or bar around which you can bend metal or wire. Mandrels come in a variety of shapes and sizes. Some are made specifically for bracelets, rings, and making bezels. Almost anything can be used as a mandrel to shape wire, including wooden dowels, ballpoint pens, chopsticks, knitting needles, carpenter's pencils, and other pieces of wire. A Sharpie-brand permanent marker is the perfect shape for making French ear wires.

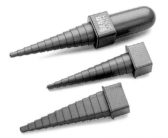

Mandrel with interchangeable shapes

Assorted mandrels

Pen and Sharpie

MANUAL COILING TOOLS: For a quick alternative to hand coiling wire around another wire, there are several handheld coiling tools. They come with a variety of different-sized mandrels and enable you to make long or short coils you can then cut to the length you need. Follow the manufacturer's instructions for the tool you choose.

ELECTRIC COILING TOOLS: Handheld electric drills used with a metal mandrel inserted in the chuck have become the tool of choice for fast and easy coiling of wire. There are also specialty electric tools made specifically for wire coiling that come with a variety of different-sized mandrels. They are particularly useful if you are making lots of jump rings for chain maille.

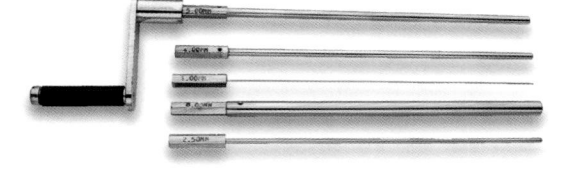

WIRE JIGS: A wire jig is a specialty wire-shaping tool made for creating consistent loops and bends. It is a small board that holds a variety of different-sized pegs. It is very useful for creating complex filigree-type components and multiple, consistent shapes. It comes in both plastic and metal.

HAMMERING TOOLS & ACCESSORIES

BALL-PEEN HAMMER: Another staple in the studio, this hammer has one round domed head and one round flat head. The domed head is used for making little dents for texture, while the flat head is used for flattening wire.

BRASS-HEAD MALLET: A brass-head mallet is used for forming, bending, and shaping. It also strikes a nice, even blow when used with stamping tools. The head is brass and therefore softer than steel. You will see damage to the flat surface of the hammer after using it with your stamps; this is to be expected.

CHASING HAMMER: Originally intended to strike other tools such as stamps and stakes, a chasing hammer is often used interchangeably with a ball-peen hammer. It has one flat head and one rounded head.

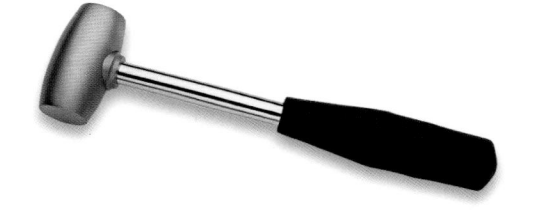

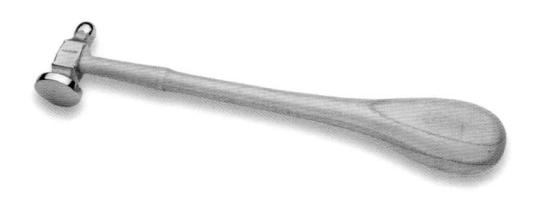

NYLON MALLET: Nylon mallets have heads made of high-impact nylon that will not mar metal. They're used for shaping metal around mandrels and for work-hardening without flattening the wire.

RAWHIDE MALLET: A hammer made of rawhide can be used on metal and wire without marring it. It's good for tapping wire into place or for hardening wire.

RIVETING HAMMER: This hammer has one round face and one chiseled face and is used for lightweight forming, texturing, and precision hammering for making wire into rivets.

TEXTURING HAMMERS: Almost any hammer can be used to add texture to your metal, like the ball side of your ball-peen hammer. There are also specialty hammers made for the express purpose of adding texture. These hammer faces make designs such as dots or checkerboards in your metal.

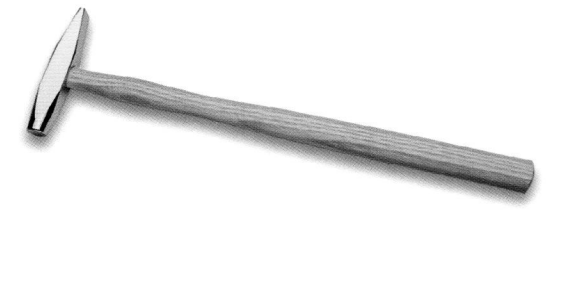

ANVIL: This handy bench tool comes in a selection of sizes. Made of hardened tool steel, it offers a flat surface and often one flat horn and one rounded horn, used for shaping and forming wire and metal.

NYLON & RUBBER BENCH BLOCKS: Nylon and rubber bench blocks provide a softer surface on which to hammer, which prevents the metal from being marred.

STEEL BENCH BLOCK: A steel bench block provides a small and portable hard surface on which to hammer wire. It's made of polished steel and is usually only ¾" (2 cm) thick and a few inches square. Use a steel bench block with a ball-peen hammer for flattening or texturing wire.

LEATHER SANDBAG: This sound-deadening and shock-absorbing pad sits beneath your bench block.

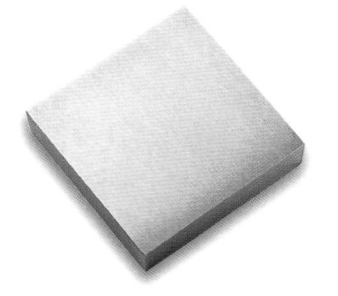

> **TIP:** A mouse pad makes a quick and handy alternative to a leather sandbag.

PIERCING TOOLS & PUNCHES

AWL: This common household tool comes in handy in a wire studio. A very sharp-pointed tool, an awl often has a wooden or acrylic ball for a handle. Use it with a hammer to punch holes in flattened wire.

HOLE-PUNCHING PLIERS: These pliers work exactly like a paper hole-punch and work best on 20-gauge and thinner. They come in various hole sizes that match up with certain wire gauges.

SCREW-DOWN HOLE-PUNCH: This tool has two drill punches that you manually twist down to create a hole. The drill on one side makes a 2 mm hole, and the drill on the other side makes a 2.3 mm hole. The 2 mm hole accommodates up to 14-gauge wire, and the 2.3 mm hole accommodates up to 12-gauge wire.

ROTARY TOOLS AND DRILL BITS: Two popular jewelry drills are the Dremel rotary tool and the flex shaft. These tools hold a variety of drill bit sizes, allowing a much larger variation in drilled hole sizes.

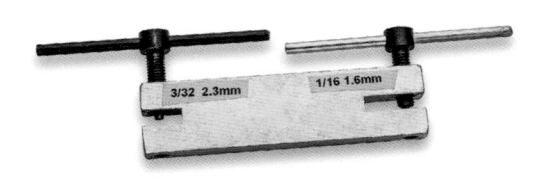

Drill bit to wire gauge conversion chart

AWG/B & S	Millimeters	Inches/Decimal	Inches/Fraction	Drill Size
0	8.26	0.325	$21/64$	n/a
1	7.34	0.289	$9/32$	n/a
2	6.52	0.257	¼	n/a
3	5.81	0.229	$7/32$	1
4	5.18	0.204	$13/64$	6
5	4.62	0.182	$3/16$	15
6	4.11	0.162	$5/32$	20
7	3.66	0.144	$9/64$	27
8	3.25	0.128	$1/8$	30
9	2.90	0.114		n/a
10	2.59	0.102		38
11	2.31	0.091	$5/32$	43
12	2.06	0.081	$5/64$	46
13	1.83	0.072		50

Drill bit to wire gauge conversion chart

AWG/B & S	Millimeters	Inches/Decimal	Inches/Fraction	Drill Size
14	1.63	0.064	$1/16$	51
15	1.45	0.057		52
16	1.30	0.051		54
17	1.14	0.045	$3/64$	55
18	1.02	0.040		56
19	0.914	0.036		60
20	0.812	0.032	$1/32$	65
21	0.711	0.028		67
22	0.635	0.025		70
23	0.558	0.022		71
24	0.508	0.020		74
25	0.457	0.018		75
26	0.406	0.016	$1/64$	77
27	0.355	0.014		78
28	0.304	0.012		79
29	0.279	0.011		80
30	0.254	0.010		n/a

TWISTING TOOLS

PIN VISE: This small tool has an adjustable chuck made to hold drill bits and cup burs. It can also be used to hold wire for twisting.

HAND DRILL: Used to manually twist your wire at a slow, controlled speed, it works best with finer gauge wire, such as 20-gauge and higher.

BENCH VISE: This vise has many uses, but it also works well to hold the ends of your wire tight as you twist it.

ELECTRIC DRILL: Using an electric drill with variable speeds and a keyless chuck is a great way to twist all gauges of wire quickly and easily.

FILING & FINISHING TOOLS

CUP BUR OR WIRE-ROUNDER: Like drill bits, burs are small tools that are inserted into a pin vise or electric rotary tool. They are cup-shaped files made to smooth the edges of a sharp end of wire and for cutting and polishing small jewelry parts. They come in a variety of sizes, and you should use one just slightly larger than the gauge of the wire you want to smooth. They are sometimes referred to as a wire rounder or wire smoother.

HAND FILES: Jeweler's files come in a variety of sizes, shapes, and cuts (coarseness). The lower the cut number, the coarser the file; #000 is the coarsest. Often a #2 file is considered a good general file, but a set of shapes and coarseness is good to have on hand. Match the shape of the file to the contour of the piece you're working on.

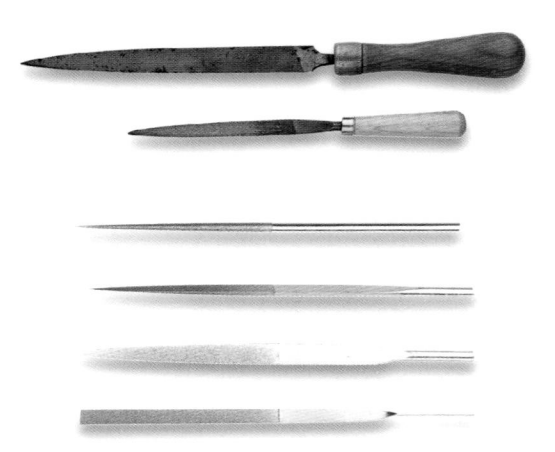

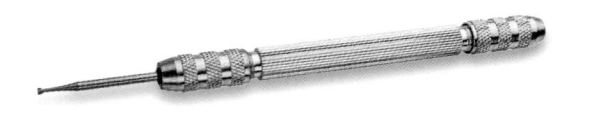

ARKANSAS SHARPENING STONE: A natural hard stone used for sharpening tools, it is perfect for deburring and hand-smoothing the ends of wire.

SANDPAPER: Sandpaper comes in a variety of grits for final finishing, including sanding off sharp burrs and fine smoothing. The smaller the number grit, the coarser the sandpaper.

PATINA & POLISHING TOOLS

PATINA: Patina refers to the changing colors that occur naturally or intentionally on the surface of metal. There are different chemicals available to create colored patinas, JAX Green, for example, or Midas Blue. You can also create patinas on certain metals with fire (see Flame Patina, page 85).

SMALL WIRE TASK BASKET: This small wire mesh basket has a handle and is used to hold small components while dipping in patina or liver of sulfur.

DARKENING SOLUTIONS: Liver of sulfur is a chemical traditionally used to darken silver, although it also works on copper and bronze. It comes in a liquid, gel, or solid chunk form and has a strong odor. There are other darkening agents (hydrochloric acid solutions) under the brand names of Silver Black, Black Max, and Black Magic. These solutions are much more toxic than liver of sulfur. For all of these products, always follow the manufacturer's guidelines.

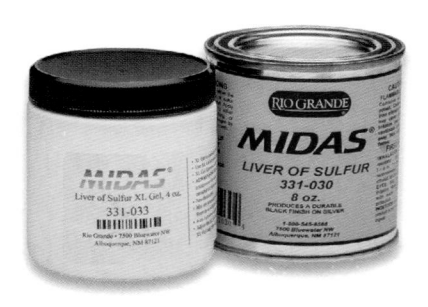

STEEL WOOL: Superfine 0000 steel wool is great for cleaning your wire before working with it. It can simultaneously clean, straighten, and polish. It's also used for removing liver of sulfur oxidation prior to final tumbling.

POLISHING CLOTH/PAD: Jewelry polishing cloths are infused with a polishing compound and can be used for cleaning wire, eliminating tarnish, and hardening wire—pulling wire through the cloth repeatedly will stiffen, or work-harden, it. Pro-Polish polishing pads are also popular.

ROTARY TUMBLER: Often associated with rock tumbling, this same electrical piece of equipment can be used to polish wire and metal jewelry. The barrel must be filled with a tumbling medium such as mixed stainless steel shot (available from a jeweler's supplier), water, and a bit of burnishing compound or non-ultra liquid dish detergent). The tumbling action against the shot polishes the metal or wire to a high shine. The tumbling action also helps work-harden, or stiffen, the wire.

STAINLESS STEEL MIXED SHOT: Used in jewelry tumblers for final high shine, stainless steel shot comes in several shapes. The weight of stainless steel, combined with the mixed shapes, makes it a good choice for polishing uniformly on complex shapes. A standard rotary tumbler uses 2 pounds of mixed stainless steel shot.

BURNISHING COMPOUND: This special formulation is added to tumblers to keep the tumbling solution clean and produce the finest shine on metal.

GILDERS PASTE: Gilders Paste is a topical colorant used on metal for a surface effect. It comes in a variety of colors that transfer directly to the metal.

RENAISSANCE WAX: Renaissance Wax was first used to preserve artifacts in the British Museum. Jewelers use this wax to protect their jewelry from tarnish and corrosion.

FLAME-WORKING TOOLS

See page 82 for Safety First!

MICRO TORCH: A handheld butane torch has a fine-point, adjustable flame that reaches a temperature up to 2,500°F (1,371°C). There are a couple of key features to look for: a flame adjuster and a sturdy base that allows hands-free use. Torches with all-metal nozzles tend to be better because extended use can melt any plastic parts near the flame. Some models come with a safety switch, which you might consider, especially if you have children in the house. To protect your eyes, wear flame-safety goggles. Most micro torches have a burn time of about 30 minutes on one tank of fuel. Fuel for the torch costs about $4 a can. It's recommended that you buy butane fuel that is triple refined and sold with the torch or at jewelry-supply stores. Lighter fuel may clog the torch and result in an uneven flame.

MINIFLAM TORCH: These specialty small handheld torches use a custom-mixed fuel and reach higher temperatures than butane torches.

SOLDERING BLOCK & SOLDERITE PAD: A soldering block, charcoal block, or Solderite pad provides a flame-resistant surface for use with a torch. It will protect your work surface from burning. The charcoal block reflects heat back onto the piece for faster fusing and soldering. It is also recommended that you place these items on a cookie sheet or large ceramic tile before working with fire.

QUENCHING BOWL: This is a ceramic, glass, or metal bowl filled with cold water. Submerging the hot metal into cold water reduces the heat of an item that has been fused, soldered, or annealed.

UTILITY PLIERS: These are everyday needle-nose pliers with a heat-resistant handle. They are not used for jewelry making but for holding wire in the flame when fusing and to dip items in the quenching bowl.

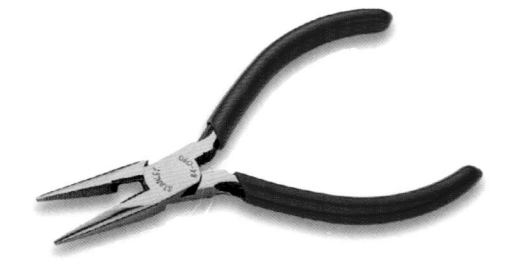

MISCELLANEOUS TOOLS

TOOL MAGIC: A rubber coating for the jaws of your pliers to protect your work from nicks and marring, Tool Magic comes in a liquid form that you dip your pliers into and allow to dry. It can be easily removed and reapplied when you need it.

LOW-STICK OR PAINTER'S TAPE: This multipurpose tool in wireworking is often used for taping pieces of wire together to insert into drill chucks for twisting or taping several pieces of wire together as you work with them. It is also frequently used to wrap the jaws of pliers to prevent marring your wire.

ANTITARNISH STRIPS: These chemically treated pieces of paper prevent tarnish when stored with your wire or jewelry in a sealed container.

PERMANENT MARKER/SHARPIE: This is used for marking tools and wire measurements, and as a mandrel when making ear wires and other bends. Marks from a Sharpie can be rubbed off with rubbing alcohol or a jewelry cleaning cloth.

THE BEGINNER'S WIREWORKING TOOLBOX

- Round-nose pliers
- Chain-nose pliers, 2 pairs
- Flat-nose pliers
- Nylon-jaw pliers
- Flush cutters
- Awl
- Steel bench block or anvil
- Ball-peen or chasing hammer
- Rawhide mallet
- Mandrels or dowels
- Needle files
- Sharpie fine-tip permanent marker
- Ruler and measuring tape
- Wire gauge
- Polishing cloth or Pro-Polish pads
- 0000 steel wool
- Liver of sulfur (optional)

ESSENTIAL TECHNIQUES

These are the fundamental methods you will learn as you are working with wire. Once you are familiar with them, you can combine and vary them in any number of ways to create unique pieces.

MEASURING

Brown & Sharpe (B & S), or American Wire Gauge (AWG), is the standard in the United States for measuring the diameter of wire. When you use a wire gauge, use the small slots around the edge of the gauge, not the round holes at the ends of the slots. Place the wire edge into a slot. If there's wiggle room, place it into the next smaller slot. When you reach a slot that it will not fit into, then the number at the end of the next larger slot is the gauge of your wire.

CLEANING WIRE

Tear off a piece of 0000 (superfine) steel wool, fold it around your wire, and pull the wire through the steel wool to clean it.

STRAIGHTENING WIRE

Pulling a piece of wire through nylon-jaw pliers will straighten any bends in the wire. Grasp one end of the wire tightly in the nylon jaws and pull with your other hand. It may take two or three pulls through the pliers to straighten the wire completely. Be aware that the manipulation of wire in any pliers, including nylon-jaw pliers, will start the process of work-hardening the wire, which will eventually make it stiffer and harder to work with. You may need to anneal it afterward.

FLUSH CUTTING

Flush cutters have two sides: a flat side and a concave side. When you cut wire, you want the end that remains on your working piece to be flat, or flush. To do this, make sure the flat side of the cutters is facing your working piece when you snip.

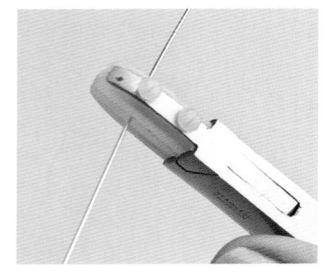

TIP: *It's always a good idea when cutting wire to wear safety glasses. Additionally, always cup your hand around the flush cutters to contain flying pieces.*

HAMMERING

Always grasp the hammer firmly near the end of the handle. Do not "choke up" on the handle as you might a baseball bat. This ensures you're using the weight of the head optimally and also keeps your hand from absorbing the shock of the impact. When hammering, be aware that you will also be work-hardening the wire. Work-hardening stiffens the wire and makes it harder to bend. You may need to anneal it afterward.

> **TIP:** Any damage or pitting on the face of a metal hammer or steel bench block will transfer those marks to your work.

TEXTURING

There are lots of tools to create texture on metal. One of the simplest is using the ball end of a ball-peen hammer. Strike the metal with enough force to transfer the impression of the hammer head to the metal and form a dimpled pattern.

STAMPING

There is a huge variety of steel design stamps available for decorating metal, including alphabets in a number of fonts. Using your bench block and brass hammer, position the design end of the stamp where you want to place the impression and give a single solid blow to the other end of the stamp. If you have a particularly ornate design stamp, use a heavier 2-pound brass hammer.

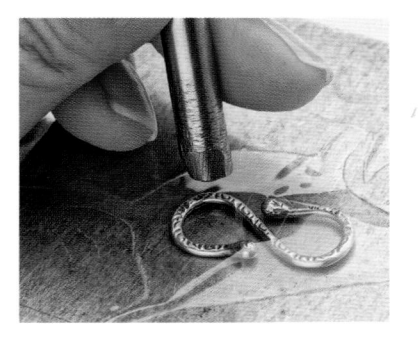

TWISTING WIRE
One Round Wire

1. Fold a 5' (1.5 m) length (or shorter) of round wire in half and secure the cut ends with tape (figure 1).

2. Place the taped end in the electric drill chuck (figure 2).

3. Grasp the wire fold in your round-nose pliers (figure 3).

4. Start the drill slowly and twist the wire until you achieve the density of twist you desire (figure 4).

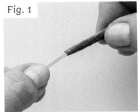

Fig. 1

Fig. 2

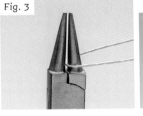

Fig. 3

Fig. 4

Two Round Wires

1. If you are twisting two separate round wires together (for example: twisting copper and silver together), always make sure they are the same gauge. Twisting different gauges together can stress the wires and lead to breaking. Tape one end of the wires together and secure in the drill chuck. On the other end, hand-twist the wires together like a twist tie *(figure 1)*.

2. Slip the twist-tie end onto your round-nose pliers *(figure 2)*.

3. Start the drill slowly and twist the wire until you achieve the density of twist you desire *(figure 3)*.

> **TIP:** Round wire must be twisted with another wire (or folded in half) to produce the twisted pattern. Twisting a single strand of square or triangular wire will produce a visible twist.

Fig. 1

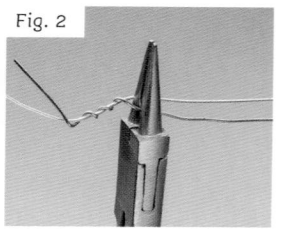

Fig. 2

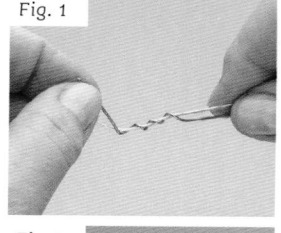

Fig. 3

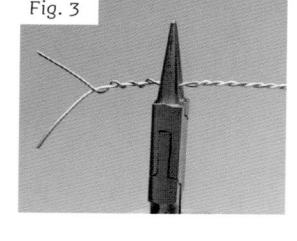

One Square Wire

1. If you are twisting one length of square wire, you don't need to tape the end that goes into the chuck unless the wire is very fine *(figure 1)*.

2. Using chain-nose pliers, make a slight bend in the other end of the square wire. Grasp that end with the chain-nose pliers and start the drill slowly until you achieve the density of twist you desire *(figure 2)*.

TIP: If you are working with longer lengths or heavier gauge wire, secure one end of the wires in a bench vise and tape the other ends to secure in the drill chuck. Another way is to screw a cup hook into your bench or the wall, slip the fold or the twist-tied ends onto the hook, and slip the taped ends into your drill chuck. If you use the hand drill, use the cup hook or bench vise, so both hands are free to crank the drill. Twisting wire work-hardens it, so it's best to anneal heavier gauge wire before you use it (see page 84).

Fig. 1

Fig. 2

Examples of twisted wires

PIERCING

1. If wire has been flattened, you can pierce it with an awl to make a hole for connecting other elements, such as ear wires. It's best to work on a scrap piece of wood. Take a sharp awl and position it where you want the hole. Push firmly to make an impression—a starter spot (*figure 1*).

2. Place the point of the awl in the impression and strike the top sharply with a hammer (*figure 2*). File any rough edges on the back of the hole, if necessary.

PUNCHING
Hole-Punch Pliers

1. Mark a dot with your permanent marker at the spot where you want the hole. Using the hole-punch pliers like a paper-punch, squeeze the handle and punch out the hole. Use only on 20-gauge metal or thinner.

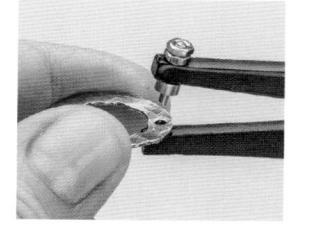

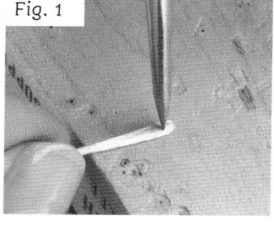

Fig. 1

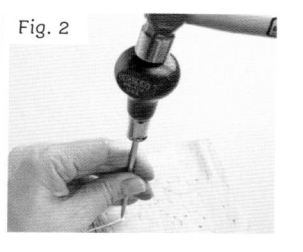

Fig. 2

Screw-Down Hole Punch

1. A screw-down punch can accommodate up to 16-gauge. Mark where you want the hole, place it under the screw, and gently screw down until you have the drill right over the dot. Eyeball the placement to make sure it's where you want it. Continue screwing down just until you feel the drill pop through; you will feel the turning get easier.

2. Don't overscrew as this could mar your metal. Begin turning in the opposite direction to release your metal. Never pull your metal off of the screw or you may damage the tip. The scrap should drop out of the bottom of the punch; if it doesn't, use a tool to pop it through.

FILING

The teeth of all metal files are made to cut only in one direction. Place the file against your metal and push the file away from you. For every stroke, pick up the file again, place it back on the metal, and push it away. These files are not made to be used like fingernail files with a back-and-forth motion.

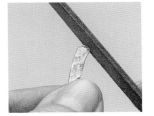

ADDING PATINA

Wash your jewelry with soap and water and dry before applying patina. It is important to remove any residual oils or fingerprints so the patina will adhere to the metal. Work in a well-ventilated area.

Liver of sulfur is one method used to darken or patina wire or metal. Dissolve a small lump of liver of sulfur in very hot water.

1. Dip your piece into the solution *(figures 1 and 2)*. The temperature of the water, the length of time you leave it in, the age of the liver-of-sulfur chunks, and the type of silver you're using all affect the color you get from the solution. You can get beautiful blues, pinks, and purples, along with the usual black.

2. Remove the piece when it reaches the desired color *(figure 3)*.

Fig. 1
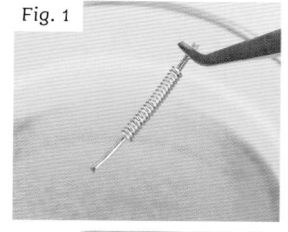

Fig. 2
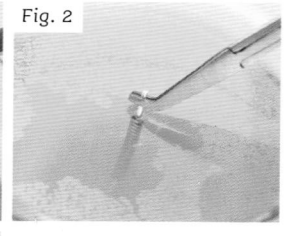

Fig. 3
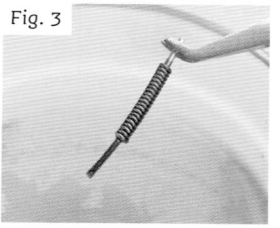

TIP: If you are oxidizing small beads or jump rings, string them onto a fine-gauge piece of wire of the same metal and twist the wire shut like a twist tie, then dip the wire into the liver of sulfur solution.

3. Dry and polish it lightly to remove some of the patina *(figure 4)* but leave the dark color in the recesses of the piece *(figure 5)*.

If you use liquid or gel liver of sulfur or another form of patina, follow the manufacturer's instructions.

Fig. 4

Fig. 5

63

Essential Techniques

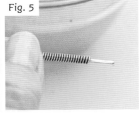

TIP: Do not put copper and silver in the same liver of sulfur solution. Copper affects the chemical balance of the solution, and if you put silver into a solution that has had copper in it, it will turn the silver a yellowish color. If your piece has silver and copper elements, you should patina the wires separately before you make the piece.

TIP: Using an electric mug warmer helps keep your liver of sulfur solution warm and active.

TUMBLE POLISHING

Place 1–2 pounds of mixed-shaped stainless steel shot in the barrel of the tumbler. Add enough water to cover the shot plus 1" (2.5 cm), a pinch of liquid dish detergent (non-ultra) or burnishing compound, and your piece of jewelry. Seal the barrel and tumble for 1–2 hours. Drain the water through a fine-mesh sieve and remove your pieces. Rinse the jewelry and the shot with clear water. Dry the jewelry. Spread the shot out on a dish towel to dry; never put away wet.

> **TIP:** Before tumbling, clean your oxidized jewelry with a polishing cloth or fine steel wool to remove some of the blackening agent. Otherwise, the tumbling will just shine the blackened color into a gunmetal appearance rather than an antiqued appearance with polished highlights.

BASIC WIREWORKING

The following techniques are used over and over in wireworking design. Becoming familiar with the terms in this chapter will enable you to read and understand tutorials in books, magazines, and online. This is the basic "toolbox" of terms and techniques.

LOOPS & LINKS
Simple Loop

1. Working from the spool, flush cut the end of the wire. Grasp the end of the wire in round-nose pliers so you can just see the tip of the wire *(figure 1)*.

2. Rotate the pliers fully until you've made a complete loop *(figure 2)*.

3. Remove the pliers. Reinsert the tip of the pliers to grasp the wire directly across from the opening of the loop. Make a sharp 45° bend across from the opening *(figure 3)*.

4. Center the loop over the length of the wire like a lollipop *(figure 4)*.

Fig. 1

Fig. 2
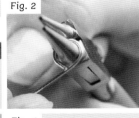

Fig. 3

Fig. 4
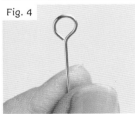

Simple Loop Link

1. Working from the spool, flush cut the end of the wire. Slip your bead onto the wire and make a simple loop at the end *(figure 1)*.

2. Use a permanent marker to mark your pliers at the spot where you made your first simple loop *(figure 2)*.

3. Slide the bead up to the loop and measure ¾" (2 cm) from the bead; flush cut the wire from the spool *(figure 3)*. (Depending upon the size of your first loop, ¾" [2 cm] may be too long.)

4. Grasp the tip of the wire at the mark you made on your pliers. The wire should be flush with the top of the jaws, and you should not be able to feel it with your fingers *(figure 4)*.

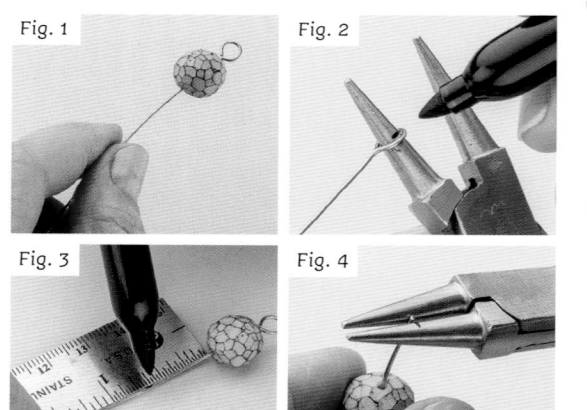

Fig. 1   Fig. 2

Fig. 3   Fig. 4

TIP: Working from the spool of wire, instead of cutting a separate length to start each piece, eliminates waste and is much more cost-effective.

5. Turn the pliers to complete a full loop *(figure 5)*. (If your second loop does not touch your bead, continue rotating your pliers until it does touch.)

6. Use flush cutters to trim away the extra coils, leaving your finished simple loop *(figure 6)*.

7. Place your chain-nose pliers opposite the join and make a 45° bend, centering the loop over the bead *(figures 7 and 8)*.

Fig. 5

Fig. 6

Fig. 7

Fig. 8

Connecting Simple-Loop Links

1. Open one loop as you would a jump ring (see page 80), opening the loop to the side, not pulling it apart *(figure 1)*.

2. Slip on your next link or component *(figure 2)*.

3. Close the loop as you would a jump ring *(figure 3)*.

Fig. 1
Fig. 2

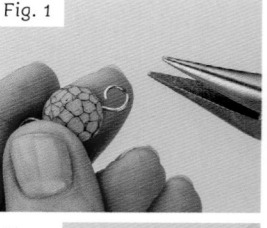
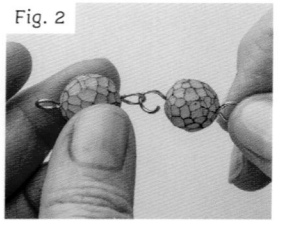

Fig. 3

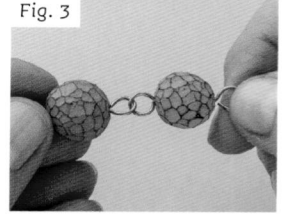

TIP: For making consistent loops, use a black permanent marker to draw a guideline on the jaw of your round-nose pliers. Use this guide to produce the same-size loop again and again.

Wrapped Loop

1. Working from the spool, flush cut the end of the wire. Grasp the wire about 2" (5 cm) from the end with chain-nose pliers. Use your fingers to bend the wire flat against the pliers to 90° *(figure 1)*.

2. Use round-nose pliers to grasp the wire right at the bend you just made, holding the pliers perpendicular to the tabletop. Pull the wire up and over the top of the round-nose pliers *(figure 2)*.

3. Pull the pliers out and put the lower jaw back into the loop you just made *(figure 3)*.

4. Continue pulling the wire around the bottom jaw of the pliers into a full round loop *(figure 4)*.

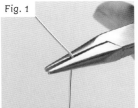
Fig. 1

Fig. 2

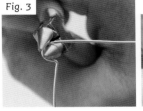
Fig. 3

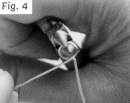
Fig. 4

5. With your fingers or chain-nose pliers, wrap the wire around the neck of the lower wire two or three times *(figures 5 and 6)*.

6. Trim the wire and pinch the end snugly with chain-nose pliers.

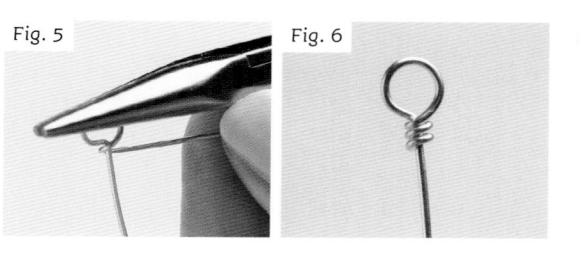

Fig. 5   Fig. 6

> **TIP:** The secret to fine-wire jewelry is neatness. Ends should be neat and smooth or tucked out of sight. And wrapped links should have the same number of wraps on each neck.

> **TIP:** Once you master a fine-wrapped loop, you can double the loop, wrapping twice around the jaws of the pliers, for additional strength and interest in your designs.

Wrapped-Loop Links

1. Working from the spool, flush cut the end of the wire. Slip your bead onto the wire and make a wrapped loop at the end. Use a permanent marker to mark your round-nose pliers at the spot where you made your first wrapped loop *(figure 1)*.

2. Grasp the wrapped neck gently with your chain-nose pliers to determine the length of the neck. Mark your chain-nose pliers at this spot *(figure 2)*.

3. Slide the bead up to the loop, measure 3" (7.5 cm) from the bead, and flush cut the wire from the spool *(figure 3)*.

4. Using the mark on your chain-nose pliers as a guide, grasp the wire at the top of the bead *(figure 4)*.

5. Use your fingers to bend the wire against the jaw to make a 90° bend *(figure 5)*.

6. Remove the chain-nose pliers. Using the mark on your round-nose pliers as a guide, make a second loop and complete the wrap *(figure 6)*.

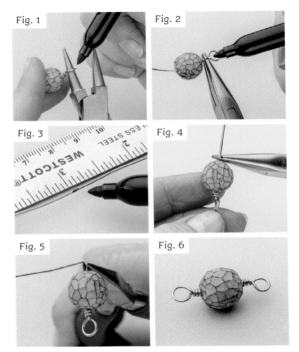

Fig. 1

Fig. 2

Fig. 3

Fig. 4

Fig. 5

Fig. 6

Connecting Wire-Wrapped Links

1. To attach a wire-wrapped link to another wire-wrapped link or component, begin a second loop on your new link but don't wrap it *(figure 1)*.

2. Slip the loop onto the next link or component *(figure 2)*.

3. Complete the wrap *(figure 3)*.

Fig. 1

Fig. 2

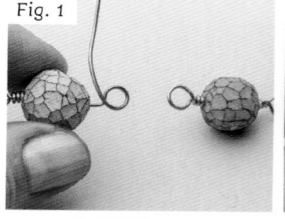

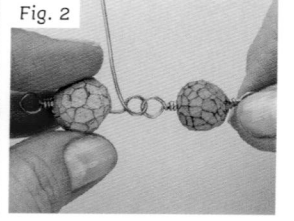

Fig. 3

Briolette Loop

1. For top-drilled stones, insert a wire through the hole and bend up both sides so that they cross over the top of the stone. You will only need a short length on one side *(figure 1)*.

2. Make a bend in each of the wires so they point straight up off the top of the stone. Use flush cutters to trim the short wire so that it's no longer than $1/8$" (3 mm) *(figure 2)*.

3. Pinch the two wires together with chain-nose pliers and bend the longer wire over the top of the shorter wire to 90° *(figure 3)*.

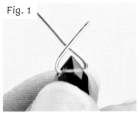

Fig. 1

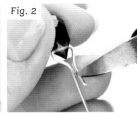

Fig. 2

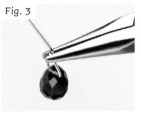

Fig. 3

4. Make a wrapped loop by switching to round-nose pliers and pulling the long wire up and over the round jaw *(figures 4 and 5)*.

5. Wrap the neck of the two wires together two or three times to secure and trim *(figures 6 and 7)*.

For another look, continue wrapping the long wire down around the top of the briolette to form a bead cap. Trim the excess wire.

TIP: Moisture is a culprit in tarnishing silver. Store your sterling wire and jewelry in an airtight container with antitarnish strips or a packet of silica desiccant (such as the little packages found in purses, shoes, and suitcases).

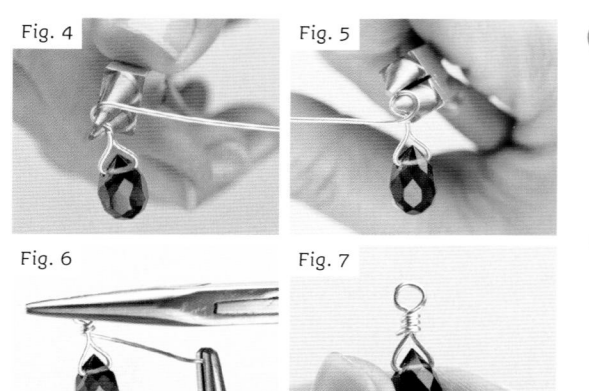

Fig. 4

Fig. 5

Fig. 6

Fig. 7

Figure-Eight Link

1. Make a loop on one end of the wire with round-nose pliers *(figure 1)*.

2. Remove the pliers and grasp the wire just below the loop you just made. Make sure you work at the same point on the jaw that you used to make the first loop so that the loops are the same size. Pull the wire around the jaw of the pliers in the opposite direction of the first loop *(figure 2)*. Flush cut the end of the wire opposite the first cut.

3. **Optional:** Hold one loop with your fingers, grasp the other loop with chain-nose pliers, and twist a quarter turn so that the loops sit perpendicular to each other *(figure 3)*.

Fig. 1

Fig. 2

Fig. 3

TIP: The flat link (shown in figure 2) works well with a clasp. The twisted link (shown in figure 3) connects nicely in a chain.

COILS

Hand Coiling

1. Coils can be made on any round mandrel, including another piece of wire. Hold one end of the wire tightly against the mandrel with your thumb and coil the length up the mandrel. Be sure to wrap snugly and keep the coils right next to one another *(figure 1)*.

2. Flush cut both ends *(figure 2)*.

Using a Coiling Tool

1. Anchor the frame to the desk using a C-clamp or hold it in your nondominant hand. Working from the spool of wire, wrap the end of the wire a couple of times around the back of the mandrel to anchor *(figure 1)*.

2. Insert the mandrel into the frame and begin turning the mandrel to start the coil, near the handle. Keep the wire taut while you feed it onto the mandrel *(figure 2)*.

Fig. 1
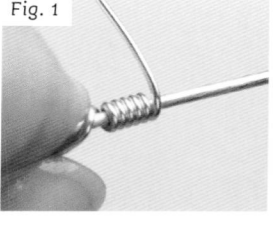

Fig. 2
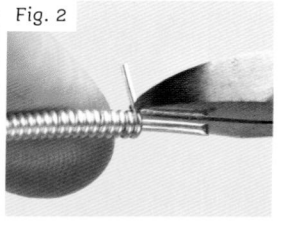

Fig. 1
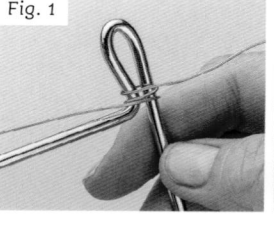

Fig. 2
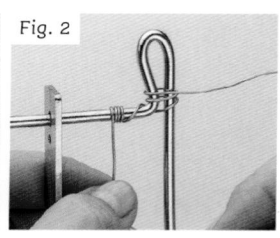

3. Gently push the coil against the frame to keep the wraps tightly against one another. Keep turning the mandrel and pushing the coil against the frame until the coil is the length you want *(figure 3)*.

4. Trim the wire from the spool, unwrap the anchor wire, and remove the coil from the mandrel. You may need to break the tension of the coil in order to remove it. To do this, grasp both ends of the coil on the mandrel and twist them slightly in opposite directions. Flush cut both ends of the coil.

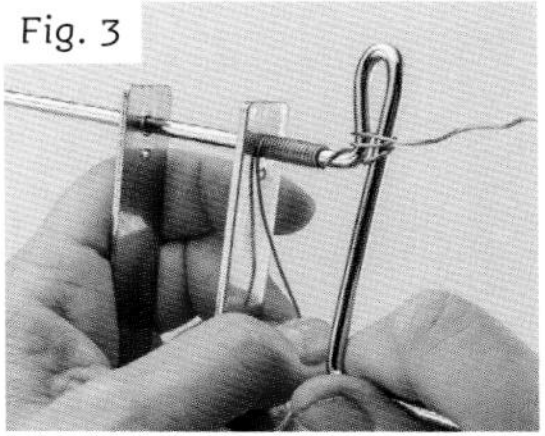

What size wire will fit through my coil:

Mandrel/Rod Size	Wire Gauge	Wire Diameter
1 mm	19	0.92 mm
1.1 mm	18	1.0 mm
1.5 mm	16	1.3 mm
2 mm	13	1.83 mm
2.5 mm	11	2.29 mm
3 mm	10	2.6 mm

Fig. 3

JUMP RINGS
Hand-Cut Jump Rings

1. Coil the wire snugly around a mandrel (*figure 1*).

2. Each single coil will make one jump ring. Remove the mandrel. Use flush cutters to cut through all the rings at the same spot along the length of the coil, snipping one or two at a time (*figure 2*).

3. They will fall away and each ring will be slightly open.

Note: *One side of the ring will be flush cut and the other side will have a beveled edge. Flush cut the beveled side so the ring will close properly. Tumble to work-harden or hammer with the rawhide hammer and bench block. The jump rings you make will have the inner diameter (ID) of the mandrel you used to make them.*

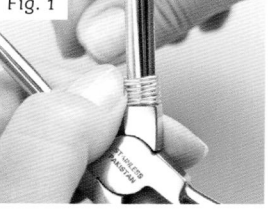
Fig. 1

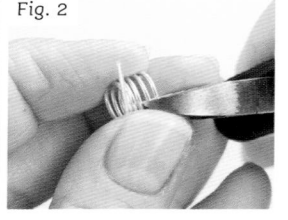
Fig. 2

TIP: If you just want to make a few jump rings, you can do them on your bail-forming pliers and hand-cut them. For a larger number of jump rings, it's easier to use a coiling tool and jeweler's saw. The advantage to saw-cut jump rings is that both sides are flush cut.

Saw-Cut Jump Rings

1. Make a short coil and place it in the coil-cutting pliers. Holding the pliers with your nondominant hand, insert a jeweler's saw and blade into one of the cutting channels *(figure 1)*.

> **Note:** *There are two cutting channels, one on either side of the pliers, for left- and right-handed cutting. Do not place the saw through both slots on the pliers. Angle the saw and cut down one side of the coil until the cut jump rings pop out of the top of the pliers and onto the saw blade (figure 2).*

2. Remove them carefully from the saw blade *(figure 3)*.

Fig. 1

Fig. 2

Fig. 3

TIP: When purchasing jump rings, note that some vendors sell them by inner diameter (ID) measurements and some vendors sell them by outer diameter (OD) measurements. The difference is minuscule and only essential if you're working on a complex chain maille design.

Opening and Closing Jump Rings

1. Always use two chain- or bent-nose pliers to open and close jump rings. Grasp the ring on each side of the opening with pliers *(figure 1)*.

2. Gently push one side away from you while pulling the other side toward you, so the ring opens from side to side *(figure 2)*.

3. To close, reverse the directions of your hands.

SPIRALS
Closed Spiral

1. Make a very small loop with round-nose pliers *(figure 1)*.

2. Grasp the loop in flat-nose pliers *(figure 2)*.

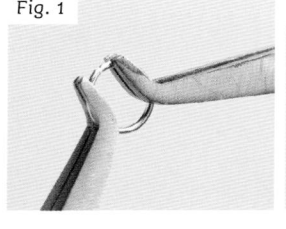

Fig. 1

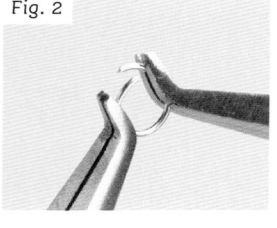

Fig. 2

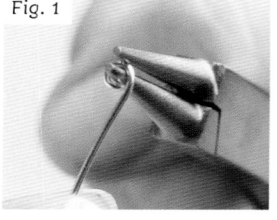

Fig. 1

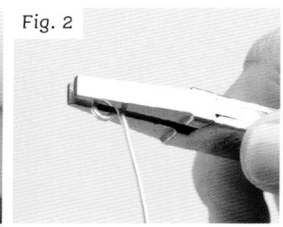

Fig. 2

3. Use the thumb of your other hand to push the wire around the loop *(figure 3)*.

4. Continue to move the spiral around in the jaws of the flat-nose pliers to enable you to enlarge the coil.

Fig. 3

Open Spiral

1. Make a small loop with your round-nose pliers *(figure 1)*.

2. Grasp the loop in flat-nose pliers or nylon-jaw pliers and use the thumb of your other hand to push the wire loosely around the loop. Continue to move the spiral around in the jaws of the flat-nose pliers to enable you to enlarge the coil *(figure 2)*.

For examples of how to use spirals in your designs, see Head Pins (page 88), Ear Wires (page 91), and Clasps (page 97).

Fig. 1

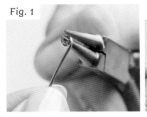

Fig. 2

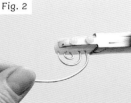

WORKING WITH FIRE

At some point in your journey of working with wire, you will discover some techniques that require flame, such as heat patina and balling up the ends of wire. All you need is a small handheld butane micro torch, and you will find that with a little practice, it becomes quite easy and unintimidating.

> **TIP:** Always read the directions before refilling your torch and make sure to turn it completely off before you put it away.

SAFETY FIRST!

When working with fire, make sure your hair is pulled back, your sleeves are rolled up, and nothing else flammable is near the flame. Make sure your fire brick or Solderite pad are on a fireproof surface, such as a baking sheet. Keep a fire extinguisher nearby. Never allow children or pets near an open flame. Don't touch the hot tools and always quench your metal before handling.

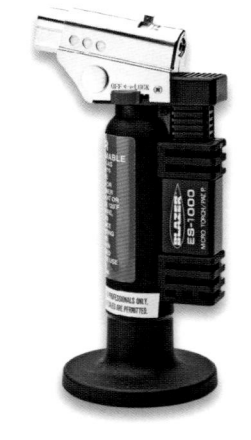

USING A MICRO TORCH

Micro torches are widely available online and in hardware stores. They all tend to burn at around the same temperature: 2,500°F (1,371°C) *(figure 1)*. This temperature is hot enough for fusing fine-silver wire as well as a lot of soldering tasks. (For more information on soldering, see For Further Reading, page 111.) When you're using a micro torch, it's important to keep the torch filled in order to get the highest temperature from it. If it starts to take noticeably longer to heat and melt the metal or solder, refill the torch. The melting point for copper, fine silver, and sterling silver are well below the maximum temperature, making this the perfect tool for fusing and soldering. Always follow the manufacturer's instructions for safety when using a torch.

TIP: The hottest part of the flame is at the blue tip inside the larger orange flame.

TIP: Refueling the torch before each use ensures that you will have the hottest flame.

QUENCHING

Whenever you are using a torch to heat or fuse wire, dip the finished piece in a bowl of water before touching it *(figure 2)*. Even if a piece is not glowing, a quick dip in a quenching bowl will ensure that you're not burned.

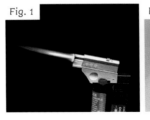

Fig. 1

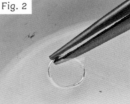

Fig. 2

ANNEALING

Annealing means heating wire or metal to a temperature at which it becomes soft and malleable. When you work with any metal for a time, it will eventually become stiffer and harder to bend. That's called work-hardening. You can restore that malleability with a torch. Run the flame back and forth several times along the length of wire you want to soften. Wire is so thin that it doesn't need to glow in order to become annealed. Use pliers to transfer the annealed piece to a bowl of cold water to quench it before touching it.

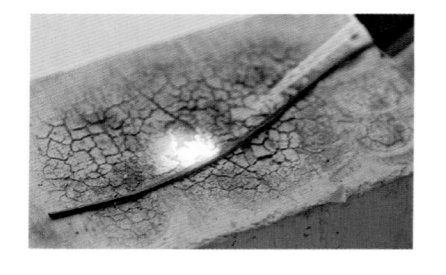

> **TIP:** Heating metal can result in fire scale, a coating of black oxidation on the metal. Fire scale can be removed using steel wool or a nontoxic citric acid–based jewelry cleaner.

BALLING/DRAWING A BEAD

1. Using utility pliers or tweezers, hold one end of a piece of copper, sterling, or fine-silver wire perpendicular in the blue, hottest portion of the flame on the butane torch (*figure 1*).

2. When the wire balls up to the size you desire, remove it from the flame, quench it in a bowl of cool water, and clean off the fire scale if needed (*figure 2*).

FLAME PATINA

Fire will change the color of certain metals. Copper, in particular, will often take on beautiful shades of red when heated with a torch and quenched. Bronze turns a warm chocolate color. In this case, you can polish the colored metal, but there will be no need to use cleaner (*figure 1*).

Fig. 1

Fig. 1

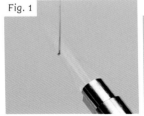

Fig. 2

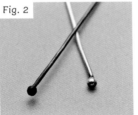

FUSING

1. Fine silver and Argentium wire can be joined without solder, unlike sterling silver, copper, and other metal alloys. The most fundamental rule of fusing is that you must heat the entire piece, not just the join where the two metal ends meet *(figure 1)*.

2. Focusing on the join alone results in just burning away the metal there. Instead, slowly and methodically rotate the torch around the entire piece until it's all very hot and then focus on the join to fuse the fine silver. Once it flows, immediately pull the flame away; the seam should now be invisible *(figure 2)*.

Fig. 1

Fig. 2

WIRE FINDINGS

Findings are the elements that connect, attach, close, or join jewelry pieces together. There are many commercially produced findings, but well-designed handcrafted findings can become your signature as a designer, complementing and enhancing a piece and stylishly finishing it off.

TIP: Silver jewelry will turn black from chlorine in swimming pools and hot tubs and from wear and tear! Remove the tarnish with silver cleaner or a Pro-Polish pad.

What gauge wire should I use?

12-GAUGE: neck wires, bangles.

14-GAUGE: neck wires, bangles, jump rings, links, clasps.

16-GAUGE: head pins, eye pins, jump rings, links, clasps, chain maille.

18-GAUGE: head pins, eye pins, jump rings, links, clasps, chain maille, coiling.

20-GAUGE: head pins, eye pins, jump rings, links, clasps, ear wires, chain maille, coiling.

22-GAUGE: head pins, eye pins, coiling, lashing.

24-GAUGE: lashing, weaving.

26-GAUGE: lashing, weaving.

HEAD PINS

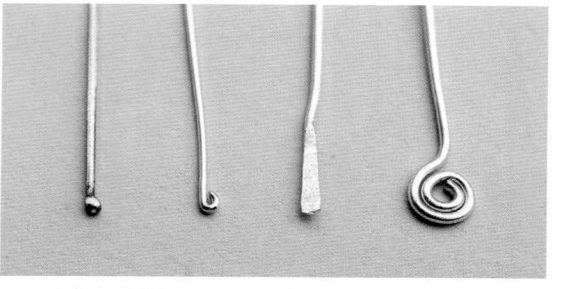

From left: balled head pin, pinched head pin, flattened head pin, spiraled head pin

Balled Head Pin

Make a small loop on the end of 1"–3" (2.5–7.5 cm) of wire. Hold the nonlooped wire end with the utility pliers and place the looped end into the micro-torch flame. When the wire balls up to the size you desire, remove it from the flame and quench it in a bowl of cool water. (To see this process illustrated, see page 85.)

Pinched Head Pin

This is the quickest and easiest head pin to make. Using any wire, bend one end up 1/16" (2 mm) with chain-nose pliers and pinch it snugly against the length of the wire.

Flattened Head Pin

Using any wire, hold one end of the wire against your steel bench block and hammer 1/8" (3 mm) flat with a ball-peen hammer.

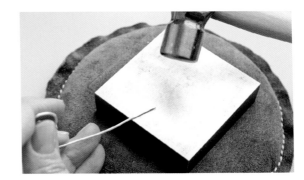

TIP: When flattening wire with a hammer, work slowly and in stages. If you overflatten the wire, you may end up with sharp edges. Also, never flatten overlapping wires as this weakens the wire considerably.

Spiraled Head Pin

1. Using any wire, make a tiny loop at the end of the wire with the tip of the round-nose pliers *(figure 1)*.

2. With chain- or flat-nose pliers, hold the loop you just made flat in the jaws and use the thumb of your other hand to push the long wire around the loop to form a spiral *(figure 2)*. When the spiral is the size you want, use your chain- or flat-nose pliers to bend the remaining wire out from the spiral at a 90° angle.

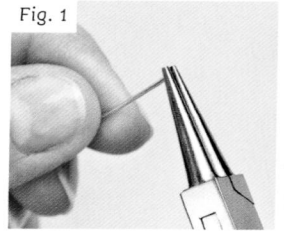
Fig. 1

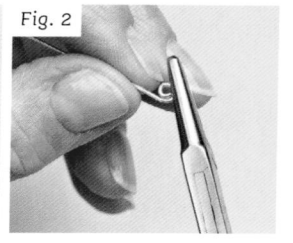
Fig. 2

EAR WIRES
Basic Ear Wires

1. Make a small loop on the end of 1½" (3.8 cm) of wire *(figure 1)*.

2. Hold the loop against a Sharpie marker and bend the wire over the marker away from the loop *(figure 2)*.

3. Use round-nose pliers to make a small bend up at the end of the wire *(figure 3)*. Use a cup bur or file to smooth the end of the wire. Repeat for the other ear wire.

> **TIP:** 20-gauge full-hard wire is best for making ear wires because the wire holds its shape. Thinner wire can sometimes be too weak, and a thicker gauge can be hard on the ears. Use sterling silver, Argentium, or niobium wire to avoid potential sensitivity if you are allergic to certain metals.

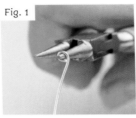

Fig. 1

Fig. 2

Fig. 3

Flattened Ear Wires

1. Hammer flat the tip of 1¾" (4.5 cm) of wire *(figure 1)*.

2. Use round-nose pliers to bend up the flattened tip into a loop *(figure 2)*.

3. Hold the loop against a Sharpie marker and bend the wire over the marker away from the loop *(figure 3)*.

4. Use round-nose pliers to make a small bend upward at the end of the wire. Use a cup bur or file to smooth the end of the wire. Repeat for the other ear wire.

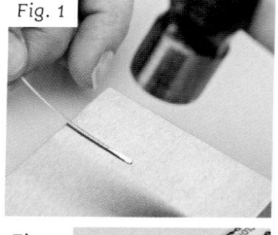
Fig. 1

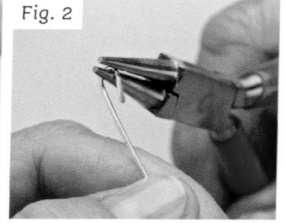
Fig. 2

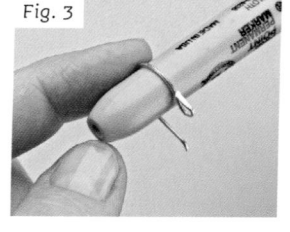
Fig. 3

Balled Ear Wires

1. Ball up the end of 1¾" (4.5 cm) of sterling, copper, or fine-silver wire as with a balled head pin (see page 88). Quench in water to cool. Use round-nose pliers to make a small loop at the balled end *(figure 1)*.

2. Hold the loop against a Sharpie marker and bend the wire over the marker away from the loop *(figure 2)*. Use round-nose pliers to make a small bend upward at the end of the wire. Use a cup bur or file to smooth the end of the wire. Repeat for the other ear wire.

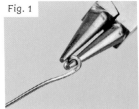
Fig. 1

Fig. 2

Spiraled Ear Wires

1. Create a spiral at the end of 1¾" (4.5 cm) of wire *(figure 1)*.

2. Hold the spiral flat in your chain-nose pliers and bend the wire perpendicular to the spiral *(figure 2)*.

3. Hold the spiral against a Sharpie marker and bend the wire over the marker away from the spiral *(figure 3)*.

4. Pinch the spiral against the finished ear wire. Use round-nose pliers to make a small bend upward at the end of the wire. Use a cup bur or file to smooth the end of the wire *(figure 4)*. Repeat for the other ear wire.

Fig. 1

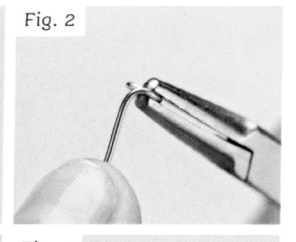

Fig. 2

Fig. 3

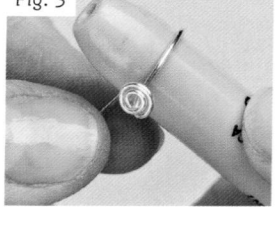

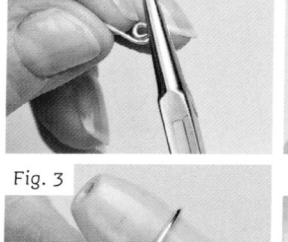

Fig. 4

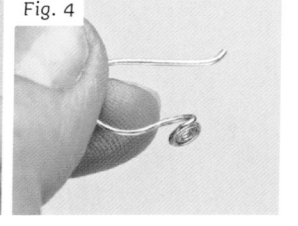

Balloon Ear Wires

1. Working from the spool, flush cut the end of the wire. With round-nose pliers, make a simple loop near the tip of the pliers. Do not center the loop on the end of the wire *(figure 1)*.

Fig. 1

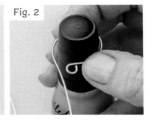

Fig. 2

2. Hold the loop against a 14 mm round mandrel, such as the top of a nail polish bottle, and wrap the wire around the mandrel until it almost meets the loop *(figure 2)*.

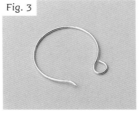

Fig. 3

3. Remove from the mandrel and flush cut the wire from the spool. Use round-nose pliers to slightly bend the end of the ear wire upward *(figure 3)*.

4. Use a cup bur or file to smooth the end of the wire. Repeat for the other ear wire.

Basic Hoops

1. Cut 3½" (9 cm) of wire and flush cut both ends *(figure 1)*.

2. Place the middle of the wire against the size 10 mark on the ring mandrel *(figure 2)*.

3. Wrap the ends of the wire in opposite directions to form a circle *(figure 3)*.

4. Use the tip of the round-nose pliers to make a P-shaped loop on one end of the wire *(figure 4)*.

5. Use chain-nose pliers to bend the other end of the wire, opposite the loop, up at a 90° angle *(figure 5)*.

6. Trim the end to ⅛" (3 mm). Use a file or cup bur to round and smooth the end of the wire *(figure 6)*. Repeat for the other ear wire.

Fig. 1

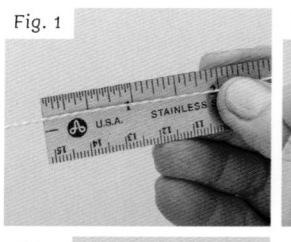
Fig. 2

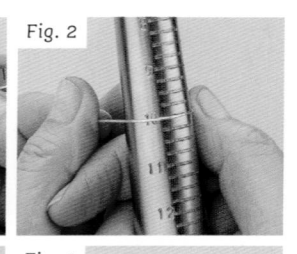

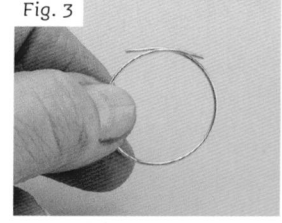
Fig. 3

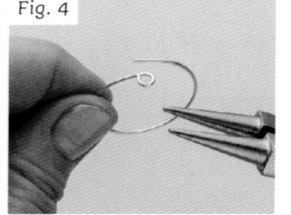
Fig. 4

Fig. 5

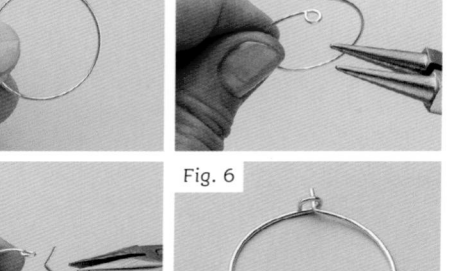
Fig. 6

CLASPS
Simple Hook

1. Working from the spool, make a simple loop on the end of the wire with round-nose pliers. Hold a Sharpie marker against the wire above the loop and bend the wire over the marker and down parallel to the loop. Flush cut the wire across from the loop *(figure 1)*.

2. With round-nose pliers, make a small bend upward at the end of the hook *(figure 2)*.

3. Flatten the curve of the hook with a ball-peen hammer to work-harden and strengthen the hook *(figures 3 and 4)*.

Fig. 1
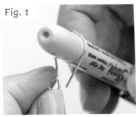

Fig. 2

Fig. 3

Fig. 4
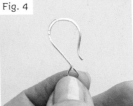

Basic Wrapped Hook

1. Working from the spool, make a wrapped loop on the end of the wire *(figure 1)*.

2. Bend the wire over a mandrel such as a Sharpie to form a hook shape *(figure 2)*.

3. Flush cut the wire from the spool, below the wrapped loop *(figure 3)*.

4. Using the flat end of the ball-peen hammer and a steel bench block, hammer flat $3/8$" (1 cm) at the end of the wire *(figure 4)*.

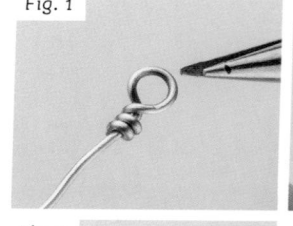

Fig. 1

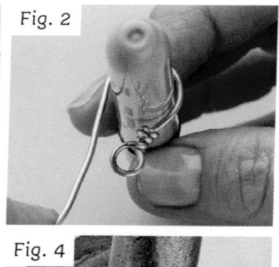

Fig. 2

Fig. 3

Fig. 4

5. Use the tip of the round-nose pliers to make a tiny loop with the flattened end of the wire *(figure 5)*.

6. Bend the wire back to a 45° angle, just above the wrapped loop *(figure 6)*.

7. Flatten the curve of the hook with the hammer to work-harden and strengthen the hook *(figures 7 and 8)*.

Fig. 5

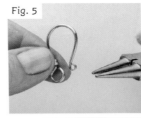

Fig. 6

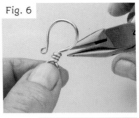

Fig. 7

Fig. 8

S-Hook

1. This clasp can be made in any size, depending on the length of wire you start with. With round-nose pliers, make a small loop on each end, going in opposite directions (*figure 1*).

2. Grasp the wire just below one loop, with the loop facing you. Roll the pliers away from you until the loop almost touches the straight part of the wire (*figure 2*).

3. Repeat Step 2 on the other end of the wire (*figure 3*).

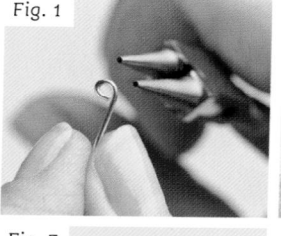
Fig. 1

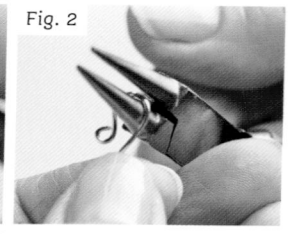
Fig. 2

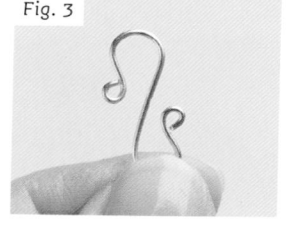
Fig. 3

Spiral Hook

1. This clasp can be made with a tight spiral or a loose, open spiral. Both begin with a small loop made with round-nose pliers (*figure 1*).

2. With flat-nose or nylon-jaw pliers, make a spiral (*figure 2*).

3. Leave about 2" (5 cm) of wire beyond the spiral and, at the other end of the wire, flatten ¼" (6 mm) with a ball-peen hammer (*figure 3*).

4. Make a very small loop in the same direction as the spiral (*figure 4*).

Fig. 1

Fig. 2

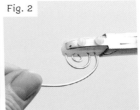

Fig. 3

Fig. 4

5. Using pliers or a Sharpie as a mandrel, bend the long part of wire into a hook *(figure 5)*.

6. Flatten the curve of the hook with a ball-peen hammer and steel bench block to work-harden and strengthen the hook *(figures 6 and 7)*.

Fig. 5

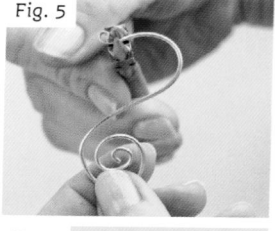

Fig.6

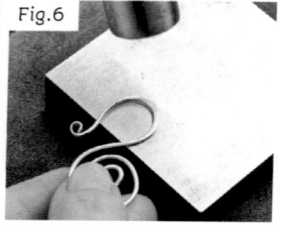

Fig. 7

Basic Toggle Bar

1. Working from the spool, flush cut the end of the wire. Measure 1¼" (3.2 cm) from the end of the wire and make a loop around the middle of the round-nose pliers *(figure 1)*.

2. Measure 1" (2.5 cm) from the loop and flush cut the wire from the spool. Trim each end to ½" (1.3 cm) from the loop *(figure 2)*.

3. Use a ball-peen hammer and steel bench block to flatten each end into a ¼" (6 mm) paddle *(figure 3)*.

4. Use a file to round the ends of the wire *(figure 4)*.

5. Use this basic toggle bar *(figure 5)* with any appropriately sized closed ring (for example: ceramic, glass, rubber, or wire ring).

> **TIP:** Mass-producing findings? Throw them all into the tumbler to work-harden and polish at the same time.

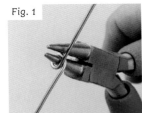

Fig. 1

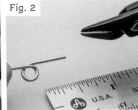

Fig. 2

Fig. 3

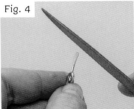

Fig. 4

Fig. 5

CHAIN MAILLE

You might not think of chain maille as being a wire technique, but every single ring is made of wire. When these rings are woven together, they create a fabric that can be simple or extremely complex. The look varies depending upon the size, gauge, and metal of the wire rings. Because chain maille is a complete art unto itself, we have only touched on it here. (For more information, see For Further Reading on page 111.)

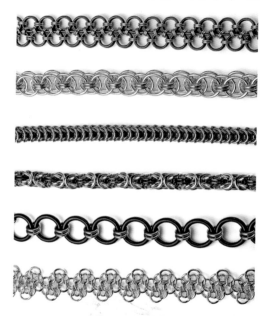

Samples by Rebeca Mojica

COMMON CHAIN TERMS

AR: Aspect Ratio

ID: Inside Diameter

OD: Outside Diameter

WD: Wire Diameter

AWG: American Wire Gauge (In the United States, includes but not limited to: copper, sterling, gold, gold-fill, Argentium, aluminum, and craft wire.) See Gauge/Size on page 17.

SWG: Standard Wire Gauge (In the United States, includes but not limited to: stainless steel, galvanized steel. Includes precious metals in the United Kingdom and Canada.)

Some chain maille is as simple as linking two jump rings to two more jump rings, and you can use any size rings and gauge wire that fit together. However, in more complex chain maille weaves, aspect ratio (AR) of the jump rings is critical. That is the relationship between the thickness of the wire, or wire diameter (WD), and the inside diameter (ID) of the ring. The AR determines how many jump rings can fit inside another jump ring. Chain maille patterns will come with the required AR or AR range for that weave in order to produce a perfectly fluid weave. Lower AR rings will produce a tighter weave, while larger AR rings will produce a looser, airy weave.

Common wire diameters

AWG/B & S	Inches	Millimeters
12	0.081	2.05
13	0.072	1.83
14	0.064	1.63
15	0.057	1.45
16	0.051	1.29
17	0.045	1.15
18	0.040	1.02
19	0.036	0.912
20	0.032	0.813
21	0.029	0.724
22	0.025	0.643

To determine the AR of the rings you have, use this formula: ID ÷ WD = AR

If a particular weave recommends a certain AR or AR range, you need to make sure your rings fit within that range. Otherwise, the weave may come out too loose or too tight. If the rings are way too tight, you will not even be able to fit the right number of rings within each other. If you find a pattern you like, but would like to make it with heavier or finer jump rings, use the basic AR formula in reverse.

To determine the ID of the rings you have, use this formula: WD × AR = ID

For instance, if you want to use 14-gauge rings instead of 16-gauge rings, and you know the AR for the bracelet is 3.29, you would multiply the WD (1.63 mm) by the AR (3.29) to get the ID (5.36 mm) size of 14-gauge rings you would need to buy.

TIP: Be careful when buying jump rings that you are using the same measuring standard that the designer has noted. Some rings will use AWG (American Wire Gauge) sizes, and some rings will use SWG (Standard Wire Gauge) sizes.

TIP: Smooth, nearly invisible joins are the key to beautiful, fine chain maille. Use two pliers to wiggle the ends together and run your finger over the joins to feel that they're closed as fully as possible.

TIP: Wear magnifying glasses or prescription glasses to reduce eye strain.

THE BEGINNER'S CHAIN MAILLE TOOLBOX

- Chain-nose, flat-nose, or bent-nose pliers, 2 pairs

- Awl or scribe

- Needle files

- Reading glasses or magnifiers

- Bead mat or towel

- Rotary tumbler

- Mixed stainless steel shot

- Burnishing compound

- Liver of sulfur (optional)

- 0000 steel wool

- Pro-Polish pads

WEAVING

Weaving fine-gauge wire around heavier core wires can create beautiful patterns and texture in wire jewelry designs. Weaving can also be used to connect separate elements of a design to each other. Shown here are some basic weave patterns, though there are many more possible as you vary the number of wraps and the number of core wires you use. (For more information, see For Further Reading, page 111.)

The key to fine-wire weaving is keeping your core wires nice and straight and evenly spaced from each other. Keep your weaving wire from kinking, weave tightly, and make sure your wraps are snug against one another.

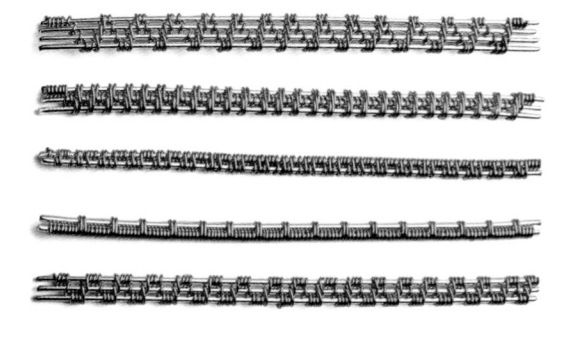

Samples by Deborah Gray-Wurz

> **TIP:** Fine-gauge wire (22-gauge or finer) kinks very easily, and you should work with shorter lengths.

RESOURCES

TOOLS

Beaducation Inc.
beaducation.com

Coiling Gizmo
coilinggizmo.com

Dremel Tools
dremel.com

Home Depot
homedepot.com

Harbor Freight Tools
harborfreight.com

JewelrySupply.com
jewelrysupply.com

Metalliferous
metalliferous.com

Miniflam
miniflam.com

Objects and Elements
objectsandelements.com

Otto Frei
ottofrei.com

Rio Grande
riogrande.com

Santa Fe Jewelers Supply
sfjssantafe.com

T. B. Hagstoz & Son Inc.
hagstoz.com

Thunderbird Supply
thunderbirdsupply.com

WigJig
wigjig.com

Wire-Sculpture.com
wire-sculpture.com

Wubbers
wubbers.com

WIRE

Beadalon
beadalon.com

Beaducation Inc.
beaducation.com

Fire Mountain Gems
and Beads
firemountaingems.com

Helby (The BeadSmith)
helby.com

JewelrySupply.com
jewelrysupply.com

Metalliferous
metalliferous.com

MyElements
myelements.etsy.com

Objects and Elements
objectsandelements.com

Paramount Wire Co.
parawire.com

Rio Grande
riogrande.com

Santa Fe Jewelers Supply
sfjssantafe.com

Soft Flex
softflexcompany.com

T. B. Hagstoz & Son Inc.
hagstoz.com

Thunderbird Supply
thunderbirdsupply.com

CHAIN MAILLE SUPPLIES

Blue Buddha Boutique
bluebuddhaboutique.com

Monsterslayer
monsterslayer.com

The Ring Lord
theringlord.com

Urban Maille
urbanmaille.com

STAMPS

Beaducation Inc.
beaducation.com

JewelrySupply.com
jewelrysupply.com

PJ Tool & Supply
pjtool.com

The Urban Beader
urbanbeader.com

FOR FURTHER READING

Bogert, Kerry. *Totally Twisted: Innovative Wirework & Art Glass Jewelry.* Loveland, Colorado: Interweave, 2009.

Bombardier, Jodi. *Weave, Wrap, Coil: Creating Artisan Wire Jewelry.* Loveland, Colorado: Interweave, 2010.

Bone, Elizabeth. *Silversmithing for Jewelry Makers: A Handbook of Techniques and Surface Treatments.* Loveland, Colorado: Interweave, 2012.

Hettmansperger, Mary. *Heat, Color, Set & Fire: Surface Effects for Metal Jewelry.* New York: Lark Crafts, 2012.

Karon, Karen. *Chain Maille Jewelry Workshop: Techniques and Projects for Weaving with Wire.* Loveland, Colorado: Interweave, 2012.

Kelly, Lisa Niven. *Stamped Metal Jewelry: Techniques & Designs for Making Custom Jewelry.* Loveland, Colorado: Interweave, 2010.

Live Wire eMagazine. Loveland, Colorado: Interweave, 2011.

Miller, Sharilyn. *Wire Art Jewelry Workshop: Step-by-Step Techniques and Projects + DVD.* Loveland, Colorado: Interweave, 2011.

Mojica, Rebeca. *Chained: Create Gorgeous Chain Mail Jewelry One Ring at a Time.* Cincinnati, Ohio: North Light Books, 2010.

Peck, Denise. *Wire Style: 50 Unique Jewelry Designs.* Loveland, Colorado: Interweave, 2008.

Peck, Denise. *Wire Style 2: 45 New Jewelry Designs + DVD.* Loveland, Colorado: Interweave, 2011.

Peck, Denise and Jane Dickerson. *Handcrafted Wire Findings: Techniques and Designs for Custom Jewelry Components.* Loveland, Colorado: Interweave, 2011.

Richbourg, Kate. *Simple Soldering: A Beginner's Guide to Jewelry Making.* Loveland, Colorado: Interweave, 2012.

Weltman, Ronna Sarvas. *Ancient Modern: Polymer Clay + Wire Jewelry.* Loveland, Colorado: Interweave, 2009.

ACKNOWLEDGMENTS

A collaboration of any kind can be a challenge, but this book was well choreographed from start to finish. We would like to thank Jim Lawson for his fabulous photographs of the tools and techniques included in this book, Allison Korleski and Erica Smith for their patience and guidance through the editorial process, Marlene Blessing for conceiving this book, Rebecca Campbell for managing all the details, Julia Boyles for her art direction, and Adrian Newman for his design and layout. And many thanks to Rebeca Mojica for her chain maille samples and Deborah Gray-Wurz for her weaving samples. Thank you all for making this book possible.

INDEX

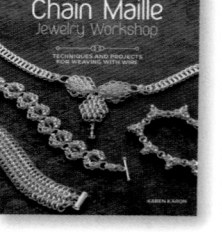

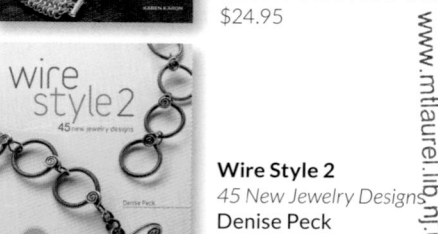
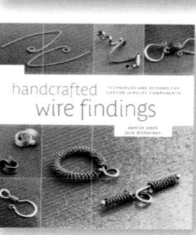
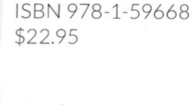